CW00730261

Josh Hara is a 1996 graduate of the Columbus College of Art and Design, where he majored in illustration. After a five-year stint as a designer for a video production company, he worked as a freelance graphic artist for clients big and small. During that decade, Josh developed a deep addiction to and affection for social media platforms like Twitter and Instagram, and turned his ability to write funny tweets into a career at an ad agency running social media programs for major brands. Since then his career has twisted, turned and evolved into more of a content strategy thing and is anyone actually still reading this…

@yoyoha

ALL THE COFFEE CUPS

JOSH HARA

unbound

First published in 2022

Unbound
Level 1, Devonshire House, One Mayfair Place, London W1J 8AJ
www.unbound.com
All rights reserved

Text design by PDQ Digital Media Solutions Ltd.

A CIP record for this book is available from the British Library

ISBN 978-1-80018-068-0 (hardback)
ISBN 978-1-80018-069-7 (ebook)

Printed in Slovenia by DZS Grafik

1 3 5 7 9 8 6 4 2

Dedicated to my wife, Halle, who has spent the entirety of our relationship taking care of all the important things while I chase every ridiculous idea that flutters through my head with a butterfly net.

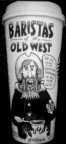

ALL THE COFFEE CUPS

HOW IT BEGAN

It was a random night in February of 2014 and Twitter found itself suddenly ablaze with pictures of Shia LaBeouf attending the premiere of one of his films with a lunch bag on his head. The 'I am not famous anymore' incident, as it came to be known for the ten minutes anyone cared about it, was his artistic reaction to the controversy he'd caused after being publicly shamed for blatantly plagiarising elements of a short film he'd released a few months prior.

As far as my artistic reaction to his artistic reaction? Well, I'd been toying with the idea of drawing on the side of my daily cup of Starbucks for a while. I don't know why, but there was something about that pristine surface that was bothering the shit out of me. That stark white, unblemished and perfectly smooth cup was calling out to me: 'I want to be more than a coffee cup, Josh Hara; deface me with your pen-fueled idiocy.'

So, carpe-ing the heck out of that diem, I recast Shia in his act of humble bravery as a cup of coffee, took a photo of it on my kitchen table and posted it on Instagram.

When I posted this cup on the left the very next day, and then a third (above), people started to notice. In fact, noted Twitter celebrity, best-selling author and all-around mega talent Kelly Oxford dropped me a note that simply said, 'I love this, I think you're on to something.'

When two of my co-workers suggested the hashtag #100CoffeeCups that was really it. A hundred illustrated cups by the end of the year felt realistic and totally doable. Three down, ninety-seven to go and I was off.

And just as this was not the last time Shia LaBeouf would challenge our perceptions of just how crazy a celebrity could act and still get cast as the lead in a Sia video, that first week set me on a course that has amounted to well over 500 illustrated coffee cups that continue to pile up on every flat surface within arm-shot.

AND NOW, THIS BOOK

I created a line of reusable coffee cups, I've occasionally partnered with brands to make a few bucks, but from the beginning, from that first moment, I wanted to make this book. Because, when I was a kid, comic collections like *Peanuts, Garfield,* * *Bloom County, MAD, The Far Side, Life in Hell* and *Calvin and Hobbes* were the first books I read by choice.

And something about this idea just worked.

This book is my 'Caffe-terion Collection', my portfolio of drips, drabs and caffeinated thoughts, fascinations and espresso-fuelled flights of fancy. Picasso had his Blue Period. This is my Brew Period. The part of my life where my doodled obsessions got to live, breathe and be posted on the internet for likes, shares, retweets and the occasional positive comment.

---

* I know Garfield has taken a lot of lumps over the years, but honestly, when *Garfield* came out it was revolutionary. He was the anti-Snoopy. A crabby, lasagna-loving, Monday-hating creep. He was the original Grumpy Cat for Christ's sake, and I make no apologies for loving that comic when I was ten years old.

BUT FIRST? SOME ANSWERS TO THE QUESTIONS I GET ON THE REGULAR...

What do you do with all the cups?

Most of them are stacked together and in a few storage tubs in my basement. Thus, I spend most of my days hoping they haven't come to life like the toys in *Toy Story* and are sitting in there wondering when I might pay attention to them again.

But, because I get this question so often, my wife recently purchased a beautiful curved glass curio cabinet – and some of my best cups are on display in our living room.

So, now I am currently consumed with new guilt over the sentient cups in the basement not lucky enough to be displayed in the trophy case upstairs.

Do you drink out of all the cups before you draw on them?

This was true during the first few months of the #100CoffeeCups project. But then Starbucks also noticed that blank panel on the cup and instead of leaving it there for the bored, Sharpie-having nincompoops, they seized the opportunity to inundate our eyeballs with their goddamned brand values.

Luckily, I was friendly with the manager of the Starbucks next door to my office, and she gave me an entire box of leftover blanks. Those have lasted me over five years.

What kind of pens do you use?

I know this likely means nothing to most of you, but this is the number one thing on most artists' minds when they see someone else's work. It's kind of like the way curly-haired people want straight hair and straight-haired people want curly hair. You always want the pen you don't have (a situation I have solved by buying every single pen ever made and hoarding them like Gollum).

But, to answer the question: I have used big Sharpies, fine-tipped Sharpies, Pigma pens (all sizes), brush pens and just about anything that will make a mark on a cup without bleeding and/or smudging. But over the last two years, I have become a devotee of the Faber-Castell Pitt pens. They are bit longer than the Pigmas and generally feel better in my hand.

How long does each cup take to draw?

According to my wife, 'TOO LONG IT'S TIME TO COME TO BED ALREADY' (laughs), but for the most part I'd say between two to five hours.

My process is to sketch the idea on paper or on my iPad, just to get a feel for what I want to do. Then lightly draw the comic with a non-photo blue pencil directly on the blank cup, then ink on top of that.

Over the years I have branched out and occasionally added colour. For some cups I used coloured pencils or Prismacolor markers, and some have been coloured digitally thanks to your friendly neighbourhood Photoshop. These take a fair bit longer, but I think the results are worth it. YOU HEAR THAT, HONEY? COLOUR MAKES THE TIME AWAY FROM OUR FAMILY WORTH IT.

Are you a coffee addict?

Depending on your definition of addict, I guess. I drink a few cups every day to keep my brain at peak performance levels. But if I lost my job would I start pawning possessions to keep my habit afloat? Yes, probably.

Are you just a corporate shill for Starbucks being paid to create these as a subversive form of advertising?

Hahahaha, oh boy, I wish.

What is your favourite coffee drink?

I drink a Venti Pike Place roast pretty much every day. That is my 'getting around' coffee. But I love Americanos, lattes, straight espresso, and I have since warmed up to iced coffee too. Basically, I am picking up whatever the coffee universe is laying down.

Do you feel reduced as an artist since you are forced to rely on a gimmick like drawing on coffee cups to get attention for your work?

This was a real, actual question I got on Instagram which haunts me to this day. The short answer is: sometimes. But drawing comics on coffee cups has given me far more than it has taken away. (My family and bank account may disagree with this statement.)

So, while I sometimes feel like a hack who lucked into a viral moment that led to a social following, I also feel lucky as hell to have done something that occasionally makes people laugh out loud or, more commonly, crack a grin while gently pushing air through their nostrils. And maybe, just maybe, I made something worth looking at.

2014
BEST OF THE FIRST

To kick off my venti-sized opus it felt best to present highlights from the original #100CoffeeCups project with my director's commentary throughout. Because this book is more than just a collection of artfully vandalised coffee cups; it's also my opportunity to blather on about my inspirations, my creative process, my childhood fear of sharks and my frustration with every *Star Wars* film that has come out since the original trilogy.

FOR THE INTERNET, BY THE INTERNET

Whether inspired by a viral BuzzFeed article like the cup on the left – which was a video of strangers awkwardly sharing a first kiss – the death of the infamous, or general celebrity shenanigans, I approached this project the same way the joke-writing public had approached Twitter. Let the internet set it up, and then have a *Cannonball Run*-style race to see who will be the first one to knock it down.

But that mad scramble only gets you so far. My best work was always a result of the way my brain stretched and pulled apart every situation from my daily life. Like one of those giant saltwater taffy machines you'd see doing its thing on the boardwalk or at a state fair.

Then, shortly after starting the project, I was off to spring break, and not wanting to lose momentum, I packed my pens and created a few cups in between long stretches of looking at my phone, digging for shells and yelling at my kids on the beach.

Upon my return from Florida, the internet decided that 24 March was Breakfast Club Day. You know, because that's the date they flash on the screen at the beginning of the movie. Predictably, I decided the day's cup should be about the hypnotic nature of Judd Nelson's nostrils. And honestly, it might be the best drawing of a celebrity I've ever done. Evidenced by the failed attempt to capture the essence of Ryan Gosling in the cup above, portraiture isn't really a strength. But like everyone, I have good days and bad days. And capturing the unending void of Judd Nelson's cavernous nostrils was a really good day.

In addition to the comings and goings of popular culture, a steady dose of my obsession with coffee has always been the foundation of this creative walkabout. Because of all the habits, vices and self-medications I have administered over the years, coffee is, without a doubt, the one that has asked the least while giving me more than I could ever expect. An elevated heart rate, stained teeth, and the occasional facial tic are a small price to pay for consistently sharpening my patience pencil and momentarily filling me with the fleeting belief that my ideas are freakin' awesome and should be shared with the world.

One aspect of this project that I don't often talk about is the 'why'. Because drawing on a cylindrical surface is no picnic. But that was kind of the point. These drawings were not going to be perfect. I wasn't going to be able to noodle them to death or scan them into Photoshop and retouch them to perfection. After four years on Twitter posting every funny thought that tore through my head flesh, I desperately wanted to return to my love of drawing cartoons. But fitting that into my busy grown-ass-man life forced me to find a way to get a comic done quickly, and with minimal impact on my family life. And by family life I mean my Netflix habit.

Now, don't get me wrong. I have pride in my work. But like the 'Weather Outside is Bullshit' comic on the opposite page, sometimes I failed to get the lettering and the drawing perfectly aligned. And that's OK. There's no way I'm scrapping it and starting again. My family's patience with my creative 'extra curriculars' had already been pushed to the limit with my incessant tweeting. So, drumming up yet another way to spend valuable time not making money was going to be even less sustainable than the cups I was drawing on.

YOGA POSES I CAN DO ———————————→

As April expelled its last winter gasp and the sun again decided to peek through the never-ending cloudiness of central Ohio, thoughts of short sleeves and bare legs began to creep into our otherwise fleece-laden selves. And with that realisation, the cups took a turn towards the long-expired New Year's resolution to eat right, exercise and hate myself for never being able to do either of those things with even a modicum of consistency over the course of my entire life.

While making fun of eating and exercise has not been medically proven to burn calories, it is a powerful coping mechanism when going through intervals of feeling physically repellent. At times like this I like to work on comics that act as a beacon to those of us who are constantly working towards living a healthier lifestyle. Because this part of life, the delicate line between health and vanity, isn't easy for any of us. Except for people with high metabolisms. And, honestly, fuck those people.

DON'T
HATE
CAFFEINATE

@YOYOHA

enjoy is extremely hot.
consumer recycled fiber.

COFFEE TOO HOT?

I made this many years ago, but somehow I still believe that if I purse my lips like a flute player and successfully get a cool blast of air through the lid hole like a proton torpedo down the Death Star's exhaust port, my coffee will miraculously become the perfect drinking temperature.

My dad is one of those people that takes the entire lid off when you sit with him at Starbucks. That feels extreme, and also cools down the coffee too rapidly. I prefer to repeatedly scald myself every few minutes until the coffee becomes drinkable, then take long drags from it like I'm Cruella de Vil sucking down a Capri cigarette.

R.I.P. ROBIN WILLIAMS

Most of the time cups are for laughs, chuckles, wry smiles or a heartfelt yet expressionless internet 'like', but the morning of 11 August was not one of those days. News that Robin Williams had died by suicide started flooding Twitter, and the world was in shock. I was six years old when *Mork & Mindy* came out and was lucky enough to be entertained by Robin Williams for my entire life.

Which makes me realise I should have worked harder on this cup. He entertained me for my whole life and this is the best I could do? Jesus. Great. Another regret I didn't even know I had. I thought writing a book was supposed to be cathartic, but like, in a good way.

Fall came and I was full on hitting my #100CoffeeCups stride. That's not to say the drawings got better because they didn't really, but I became less annoyed with the tightrope act of drawing on a curved surface and started experimenting with colour more often.

Not to mention the fact that October is my absolute favourite month of the year, not only because of Halloween and my birthday but because of… umm… Halloween and my birthday. FINE YES I AM A GOTH NARCISSIST OKAAAY.

AND THEN THE CUPS WENT VIRAL

It was the middle of November and I was about 75 cups into the 100, and while I was steadily adding to the 5,000 or so followers I had brought over to Instagram from my Twitter audience, I wasn't really getting noticed.

Remember, Instagram had really just become ubiquitous the year before I started this project, shortly after it was purchased by Facebook for a billion dollars. At that time the company had thirteen employees. THIRTEEN. That still blows my mind. And because they were still in scrappy startup mode, a big part of what they were doing to promote the app was featuring the artists and photographers that were doing cool things with the platform. I really thought if I just kept at it, they would eventually get to me.

But it had been seven months and I was getting antsy. So, I direct messaged a Twitter pal named Matt Silverman who was working at Mashable and asked him if he would be interested in writing a piece about my project.

He loved the idea and immediately apologised for not thinking of it sooner. He asked me a few questions via email and said he would let me know when it would run. A few days later, Thursday 13 November to be exact, I got the message with a link to the article. And everything just took off from there.

Instead of the daily trickle of new followers, I started getting hundreds, then thousands. And Matt's original story was getting retold on sites across the country, and then the globe.

Then, the following Sunday, BuzzFeed picked it up and over the next few days, my audience of 5,000 had ballooned to 55,000. And I'm not going to lie, it felt really, really good.

Being a writer, comedian, cartoonist, or any kind of creative expressionist is not easy. It's a world where rejection is famously the default. And, if I'm being honest, I'm not one of those people who doesn't take no for an answer. My entire life is riddled with people saying 'I don't think so' or 'we're going to go in a different direction' and me taking that feedback and using it as a reason to run as far away from that idea as I possibly can, and often in the direction of the nearest ice-cream shop.

I knew early on I was never going to be Gary Larson (*The Far Side*), Charles Schulz (*Peanuts*) or Bill Watterson (*Calvin and Hobbes*). Because when it came down to it, I just wasn't half the artist those guys were. As you peruse these cups, you'll see what I mean. Unlike those guys (and so many other talented cartoonists) I have a really hard time drawing the same characters over and over again. And that's what every comic strip in the paper had going for it: visual consistency. And that just wasn't my style.

Plus, I liked to curse and make comics about inappropriate shit sometimes.

I digress.

The point is, at this moment I had earned the one thing I had always wanted: an audience for my comics. Thousands of people that enjoyed seeing my work on a regular basis, appreciated my sense of humour, and were genuinely rooting for me to keep this weird thing going.

Shortly after all the articles hit and the viral wave had settled, I was getting contacted by book agents, publishers and by people all across the internet that wanted me to try out their new social platform or to be part of their advertising campaign.

I took some up on their offers, and most I turned down. But by the end of 2014 I had a book agent from a well-known agency in New York City and I got to work on a treatment for this exact book. The one you are reading right now. Six years ago.

Have I mentioned that I might have untreated ADHD? I'm forty-seven years old, and at the moment I am writing this I am scheduled to be tested for ADHD this upcoming Tuesday. Supposedly the process takes a few sessions, but I should find out whether my lifetime inability to focus, follow through on things, or close the cabinet doors in the kitchen is something that can be treated with prescription medication.

You know why I've never been tested for ADHD? Because I (more than likely) have ADHD and no one dialled the phone number, pressed the phone to my ear and forced me to make an appointment to get tested for ADHD.

Thankfully, I have a wife who has spent a considerable portion of our marriage shaping me into the partially functioning human being I am today. And has done so without having to purchase a handgun, though I suspect she has browsed them on Amazon to compare prices from time to time.

OK, I am getting off track – probably because I have ADHD. So, I signed with the book agent six years ago and immediately started working with Halle (Borat voice 'my wife') on the treatment. Because that's how you sell a book that you haven't written to a publisher. You basically create this multiple-page presentation to tell them about yourself, pitch them the idea, create a sample chapter or two, and reveal all the cool and innovative ways you are going to promote it and sell it to your social media audience.

And it was a such great treatment, you guys. Halle, who is the opposite of me in almost every way – organised, focused, a lawyer – helped me get it to this beautiful place. Before we started, my agent sent us treatments of books that had been sold and ours kicked their asses. Not a glancing blow, either. A roundhouse steel-toed boot kick right into their bare butt cheeks.

We were so proud. My agent was super into it. And then it was promptly rejected by every single publisher she sent it to.

Then I did what I always do when faced with the slightest bit of adversity: I gave up. I took all the good comments publishers made about liking my work and just accepted that a book of illustrated coffee cups, which would lead to a coffee cup calendar, then an entire line of @yoyoha travel mugs that would eventually be for sale at every Starbucks across the globe, was just not on the cards for me.

In short, I took no for an answer.

@YOYOHA

But I kept making cups. I finally had an audience that enjoyed my comics and that was enough for me. And maybe, if I kept doing them, they would open some alternate portal into a universe where I could comfortably afford my kids' college tuition, or better yet, buy a kick-ass speedboat.

And opportunities came. Not with Walmart, thanks to my smart-ass Black Friday *Star Wars* cup up there. But every once in a while a brand would slide into my DMs, and I would get a piping-hot pocket full of that sweet, sweet influencer scratch.

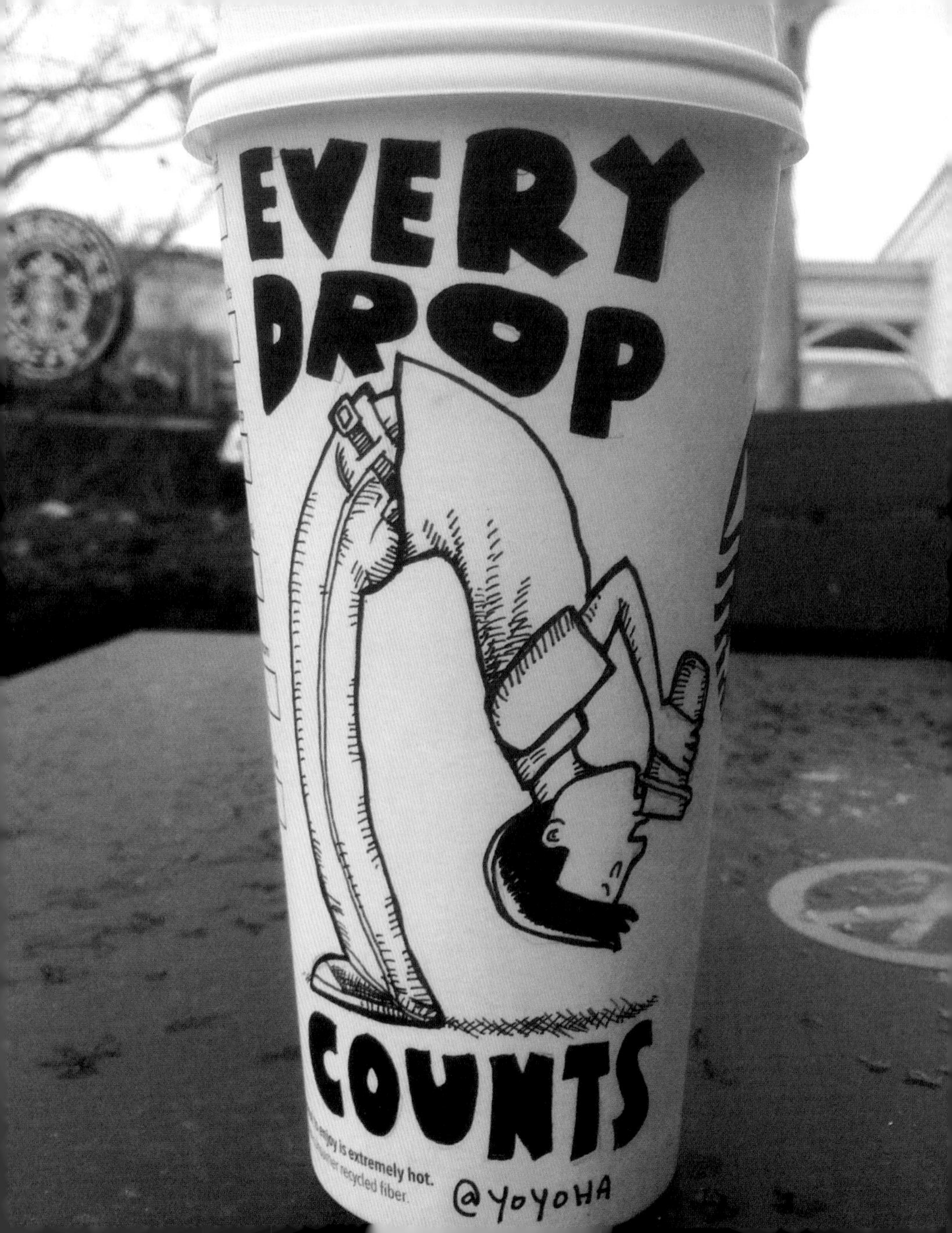
EVERY
DROP
COUNTS
@YOYOHA

THE BIG FINISH

Over the course of that December, as more articles came out and I even made the cover of the Metro section of my hometown paper, *The Columbus Dispatch* (a huge honour, I'm told), my deadline of 100 cups by 31 December was bearing down on me like a pit bull that just ate its weight in chocolate-covered espresso beans. Well, not chocolate-covered because that would make the dog very sick. So just regular espresso beans, I guess? I don't know – listen, when I agreed to write a book nobody said anything about my analogy game always needing to be on point.

Anyway, deadline bearing down on me, yada yada yada, then wouldn't you know it, somehow, just like everything else I take on, I left myself a metric shit-ton of work for the very end.

But I got there. Sure, I had to take a break from celebrating New Year's Eve with my family so I could finish my 100th cup, but my kids definitely don't remember that because they were both under ten years old and were quite drunk at the time.

I posted the cup before midnight, then woke Halle up so we could watch the ball drop and listen to Ryan Seacrest count us down to 2015. I thanked her for her patience, we embraced, then Halle went back to bed and I promptly went downstairs to make myself an obnoxiously large turkey sandwich.

As one does.

2015

JUST GETTIN' WARMED UP

The year 2015 started much the same way 2014 ended. With me eating sandwiches while the rest of my family slept, and a renewed pledge for 100 more coffee cups. Because when all else fails, keep doing your thing until someone calls the cops and they politely ask you to stop.

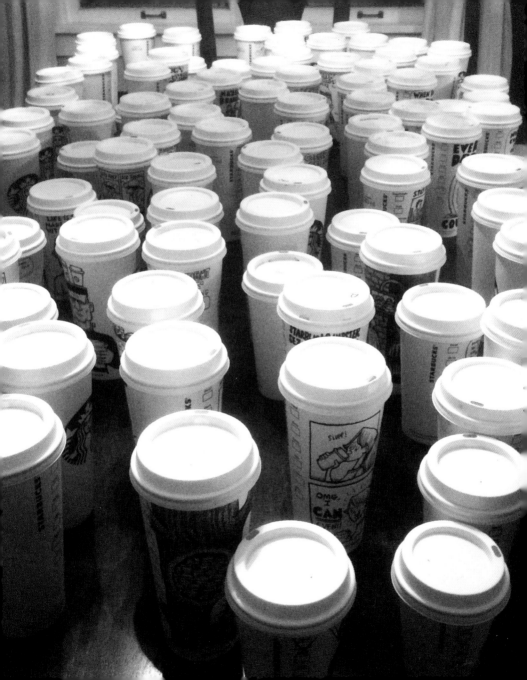

JE SUIS CHARLIE

Seven days into 2015, tragedy struck Paris when armed terrorists entered the offices of *Charlie Hebdo*, a French satirical newspaper, and twelve people were murdered. It was a horrifying way to start the new year, and artists everywhere showed their support for the victims the only way they knew how: with their pens, their brushes and their creativity. The outpouring of illustrations completely took over Instagram that week, and it really marked a time when people started seeing and sharing artwork like never before.

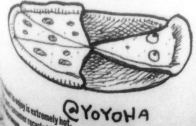

THE DRESS

As time passed, and internet life returned to normal, a new debate was about to shake the social media world to its idiot core. A photograph of 'The Dress', as it came to be known, successfully split the Wi-Fi-connected globe down the middle, half seeing it as being blue with black trim, and the other (correct/not insane) half seeing it as white with gold trim. The Dress was the first of its kind, but not the last. And it more than earned its caffeinated comic that day.

Part of the reason I can't draw the same characters over and over like a traditional cartoonist is because I'm constantly throwing an eye on artists who are better than me and trying out their techniques to see how they jive with my style. Like how to draw noses, for instance. Noses are such a pain in the ass, honestly. They are this weird shard of flesh erupting right in the middle of our faces, and when you get one wrong, it completely undermines the entire look of the person you are trying to draw. So, after I noticed a few people drawing them like flat, geometric door stops, I liked it, and tried it out for a while.

The moral of the nose anecdote is simple: never be afraid to experiment with new things. Well, except hard drugs like heroin and crack. And murder. I would also throw the movie *Duets* with Gwyneth Paltrow and Huey Lewis into this mix.

But in the realm of creative expression, I urge every artist out there to embrace the lawlessness of it. There are no rules here. There is technique, there are habits and exercises you can practise to become better. There is commitment. There is a ton of self-loathing, doubt and anonymous criticism. But there are no rules. Sometimes I crosshatch the shit out of something, sometimes I go bold and graphic. Sometimes I use my brush pen and sometimes I add colour. Because half the fun of making art is the curious exploration, or as I like to call it, the 'fucking around' part.

What's far more interesting to explore is a constant. Some creative parameter that hovers over everything you do like an old umbrella with a spoke that has come loose and invariably makes the other parents at your kid's soccer game quietly wonder when things might turn around for you professionally so you can afford a new one.

When I was first starting out and trying to figure out what to do with the internet, I reached out to Christian Lander, who created the blog 'Stuff White People Like'. Because that's what we did in the early aughts. We made blogs and hoped that our thoughts, ideas and artwork would poke its head out of the yawning chasm of the internet and somehow end up on a segment of the *Today* show. And when I showed him my blog, which was a bit of a variety show of comics, illustrations, journal entries and biting *American Idol* commentary, he gave me good feedback I have never forgotten. He said, 'I love your work, but as a blog, it lacks focus. The internet likes when you take one thing, one idea, and just relentlessly peck away at it.'

My constant is the coffee cup. Everything else – style, substance, technique, inspiration – is completely all over the place.

DAAAAAAD?

As Michelle Obama famously said, 'Being president doesn't change who you are, it reveals who you are.' I would say the same thing about parenthood. And clearly, it has revealed that I am a grumpy, selfish asshole who spends too much time on his phone.

SUN DAY ⟶

It's fun to give the Sun a little personality. Especially while fossil fuels and global emissions standards continue to pave the way for it to slowly heat our planet until the polar ice caps melt, food supplies evaporate and we have to settle our differences in a Thunderdome.

EARTH DAY!? WHY IS THERE NO SUN DAY?! I MEAN, NO SUN D—

UMM... NEVERMIND

HAPPY EARTH DAY!

@YOYOHA

@YOYOHA

Speaking of breaking rules and the general lawlessness of being an artist, I figured now would be a good time to remind people that I am almost fifty years old. Which, as far as my knees, feet, and most of the bendy parts of my body can attest, is fucking ancient.

The reason I am mentioning that personal detail is because getting to this moment, creating this book you are possibly looking at while sitting on a toilet somewhere, took me so much longer than I ever thought it would. And, if I am being honest, I haven't come close to accomplishing even half the things I thought I would have by this point in my life.

Don't get me wrong. I have achieved a lot of great things, most notably sharing a life with an amazing wife and partner, having two great boys, three adorable dogs and a job that doesn't make me want to stab my eyes out with a pair of antique brooches most of the time.

But my life has been filled with so many projects and ideas. Countless promising starts and so few quality finishes. Book ideas, business concepts, social media apps, movie scripts, a signature line of spicy roasted almonds available at grocery stores nationwide, a podcast.

I expect you think I was joking about the almonds. I assure you, I'm not. The fact is, I have yet to find a retail spicy almond that tickles my tastebuds, so I buy a big bag of raw almonds from Costco, add my special blend of head-sweat-inducing spices, then roast them to perfection. They are 100 per cent good enough to be mass produced and sold at Whole Foods. But honestly, who has the time? Instead, I will continue to enjoy them myself, occasionally bring them to work and pressure my coworkers into trying them, then chuck my dreams of being a spicy-almond tycoon on top of my unrequited-dream pile then go about my life.

My point in telling you this, dear reader, is that the age thing isn't what it used to be. And should you have some fantasy about doing something different with your life, don't let something as meaningless as how many years you've sucked oxygen out of the atmosphere get in the way of that.

Sure, there are a few territories that might not be worth pursuing after the age of forty. Olympic gymnastics, for instance, or perhaps modelling underpants.

But making stuff and posting it online? This is the one spot where the anonymity of the internet is kind of awesome. No one is looking at my coffee cups and thinking about who I am, where I live, and if I am wearing a hoody with several food stains on it (I am). Nope, I assume they couldn't give two shits about the man behind the coffee cup, they are just looking at the stupid thing I made that hopefully caused them to make a slight nose whistle.

Sometimes people like my stuff, and of course, sometimes they don't, and sometimes the algorithm doesn't let them see it because I haven't posted in a while or I've used the same hashtags too many times in a row and they think I'm some sort of bot.

All that remains is the fact that in this world, we are ageless. If you have something to say, say it, and keep saying it, until a small crowd starts to gather around and either shares your voice with others or starts a GoFundMe to get you some long overdue therapy.

ALWAYS ORDER TWO COFFEES

It's time we had a frank discussion about donuts. Yes, they are the most delicious way to spike your blood sugar levels, but why is a single donut never enough and two donuts always far too much?

I mean, what the fuck, universe?

COFFEE IS

LOVE

enjoy is extremely hot.

recycled fiber.

@YOYOHA

LOVE WINS

26 June 2015: the Supreme Court officially ruled in favour of same-sex marriage. On this day, our courts gave a long-mistreated segment of our society the same rights as everyone else. The right to love whomever they want, however they want. To see people as they are and, as a country, say, 'You belong. You matter. Your wants and needs matter. And you deserve the same rights as everyone else.' And it's heartbreaking to know that just a few years later this moment would not have been possible.

@YOYO HA

You know that scene from *Titanic* when Jack runs towards the front of the ship with his friend Fabrizio (possibly the worst representation of an Italian person in the history of entertainment), leans over the bow and into the promise of a new and better life, and as the ship cuts through the Atlantic Ocean and sun beams down on his face, he cries out for the entire universe to hear, 'I'M THE KING OF THE WORLD!'

That.

That's what drinking coffee is like.

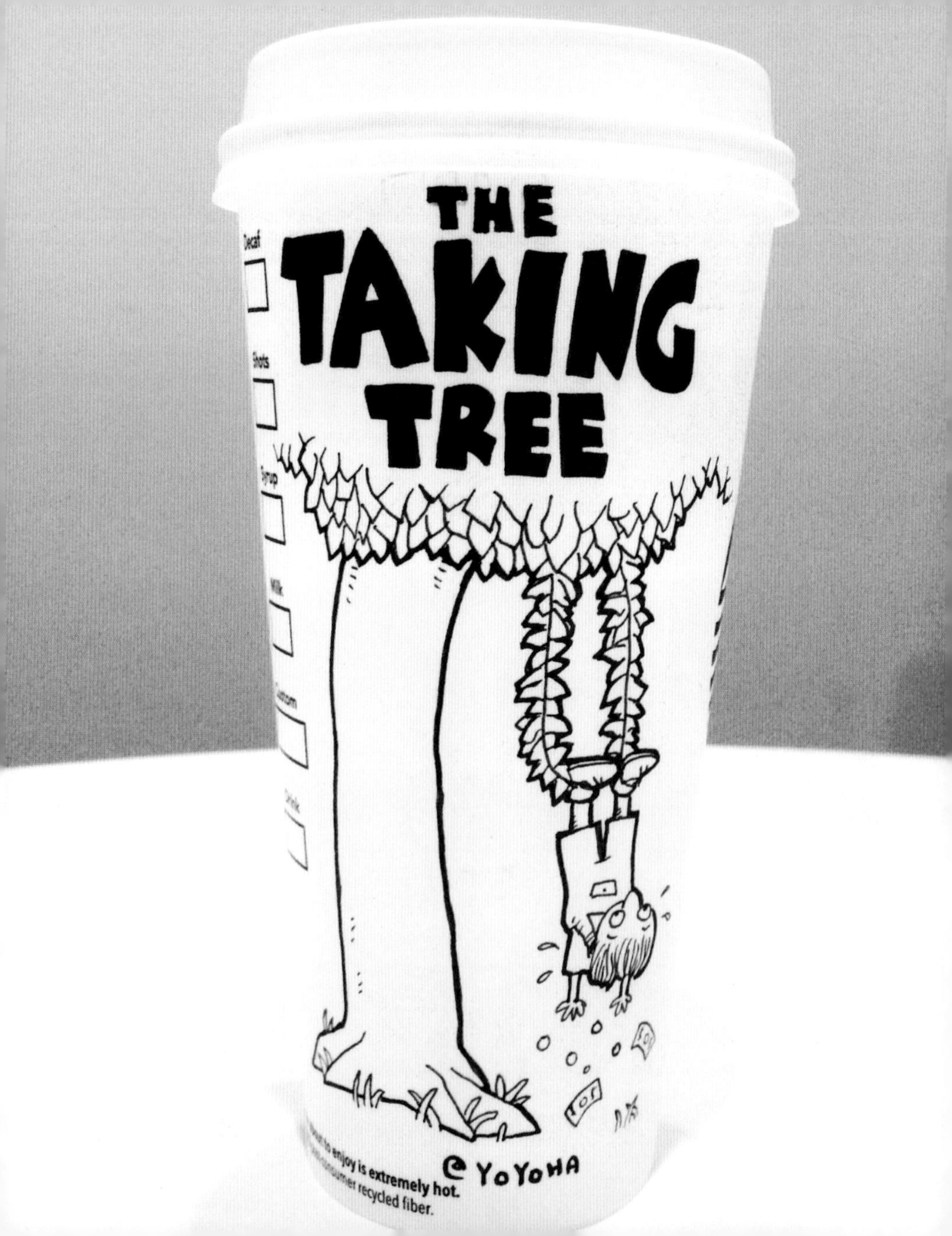
THE TAKING TREE
Decaf
Shots
Syrup
Milk
@ YOYOHA

COFFEE IS MY LIFE COACH

Every day I get up. I drink my coffee and do my best to pretend I'm not terrible. This ruse requires effort. But I often look at those around me and realise I am not alone. We all live in this pretend world together. Brains are so weird. They constantly fill us with doubt, shame and oceans of negativity. But somehow we press on. Somehow we find things to enjoy, and punch a pinhole of light through the black cloud hovering over the top of us. And coffee is there for us, rubbing our shoulders, reminding us there is light behind the darkness.

It also helps us poop.

COFFEE, ACTUALLY

All I want for Christmas
is BREWWWWWWWWWWW.

The movie *Love Actually* is kind
of weird. It's definitely the only
Christmas movie with a storyline
involving two stand-ins on a porn set.
I feel like whoever wrote that script
might have a cocaine problem.

SPOT THE PANDA ⟶

Instagrammer and cartoonist
@thedudolf had a viral moment of his
own in 2015 with his *Where's Waldo*-
esque panda cartoon. Of course his
panda was much harder to find than
my coffee panda, but mine is on the
side of a coffee cup so there.

AND A MERRY RED CUP TO US ALL ⟶

To celebrate the 2015 holiday season Starbucks released its now infamous red cup. Just a little way of marking the holiday season regardless of what you believe in. No biggie, right? Well, this was such an affront to religious conservatives that we are still dealing with the aftermath today. In light of this never-ending trench of dark divisiveness, I tried to lend a helping hand to the Anglo-Christian spectacle and remind people what the holidays are really all about. Pursing your lips and taking a pic with your BFF while you're out at the bars carousing over break.

MERRY
RED CUP!

200 REASONS TO LOVE ME

Then 2015 came to an end. J. J. Abrams had just shared his attempt to right the wrongs of the *Star Wars* prequel trilogy and, predictably, I had left way too many cups for the last two weeks of the year and I spent another New Year's Eve putting the finishing touches on my 200th cup before posting it sometime that evening. People were still liking the project, so I was fully prepared to keep going. But after two solid years, I decided to loosen the reins on the 100-per-year commitment. Mostly because I hated keeping track of them and that mad scramble at the end of the year was starting to erode the delicate walls of my wife's patience for this otherwise charming hobby.

2016

PRETEND I'M COFFEE AND HOLD ME

We should have known. Especially when the universe started permanently nopeing out some of our most beloved celebrities on what felt like a weekly basis. It was almost as if God was sparing them the pain of what was to come, allowing them to jettison themselves from the known world in a coffin-shaped escape pod, leaving the rest of us behind to toil with what felt like the most fucked-up year of our entire lives.

It wasn't all bad, of course; we had a few moments of hope and joy briefly poke their heads through the proverbial whack-a-mole table of life. But, by the end of the year, there was a collective gasp as more than 50 per cent of the nation suffered the gut punch to end all gut punches as none other than the Cheeto-dusted buffoon, Donald Trump, became the leader of the free world.

To this day I still can't believe it. I am half convinced someone invented a time machine, went back to prehistoric times and stepped on a moth and that set into motion the stupidest timeline in the multiverse.

Through it all, I still had my cups. But this year, they would provide more than just an outlet for my over-caffeinated imagination. I needed them to cope with the beginning of a four year-long anxiety attack.

FIRST DAY BACK

Being a parent is not easy, but along the way there are a few simple pleasures no parent should overlook. One of those is the return to school after a three-week winter break that feels, at minimum, a decade long by the time you claw your way to its cold, bitter end. The moment of peace once the children have been delivered back to their day jobs is as close as a human being gets to flying without one of those jet packs eighties kids were promised we'd all have by now.

R.I.P. SO MANY PEOPLE

David Bowie, Alan Rickman and Muhammad Ali died. But then Jon Snow (from *Game of Thrones*, for the few people that either hate fantasy shows or love non-conformity) was resurrected. And boy did that Jon Snow cup ignite a barrel full of wildfire from Club Spoiler Alert. I thought waiting a full twenty-four hours was enough time to ensure people had a chance to see the episode, but apparently people in Europe were only able to see the show a day later and the download times for the rest of the folks stealing the show from bit-torrent sites were unusually long.

Oh well. Live, draw, post, learn.

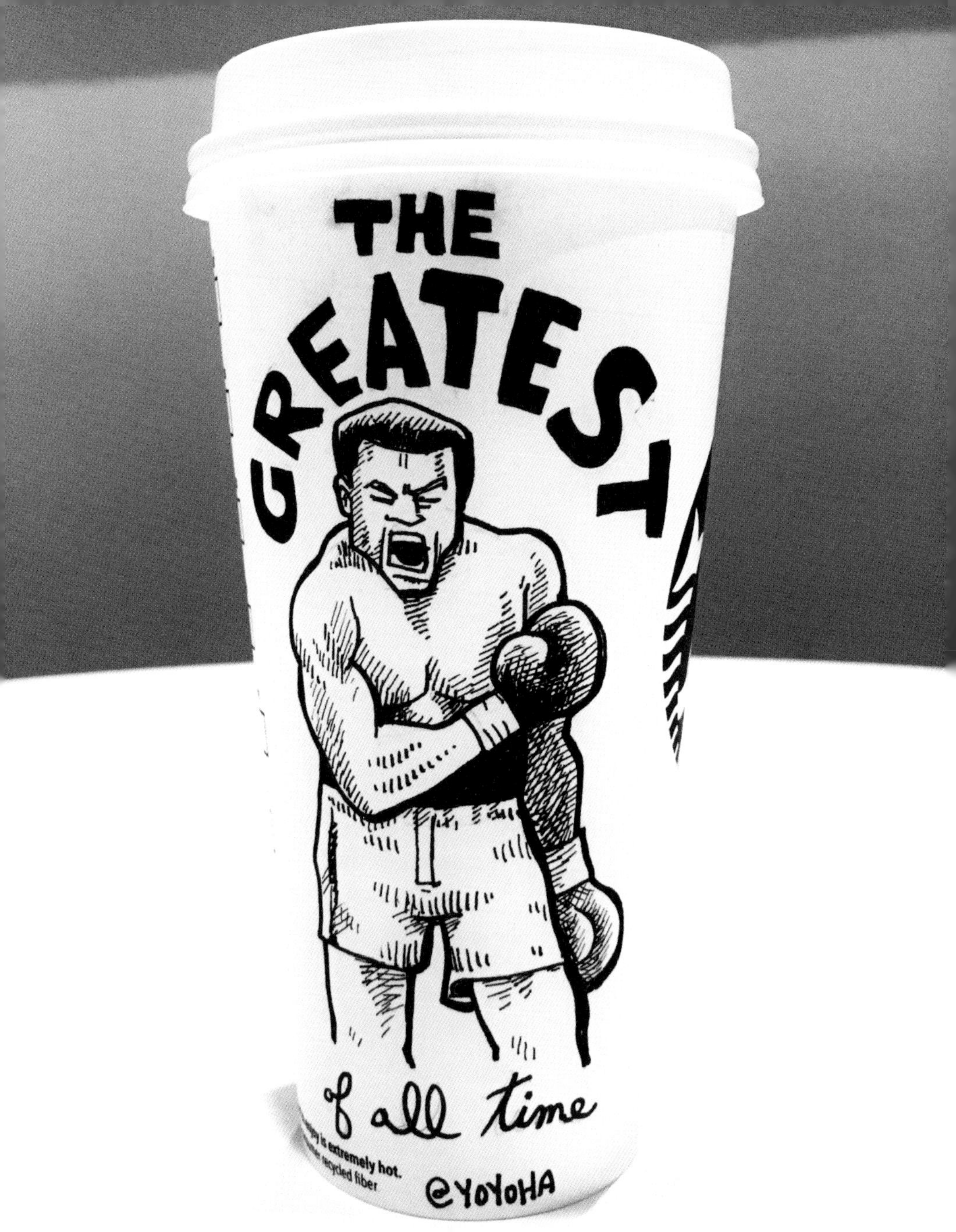
THE GREATEST
of all time
@YOYOHA

PUTTING THE 'DATE' IN *DATELINE*

We don't get to enjoy it as often as we used to, but when we aren't carting our children around from house to house, many a Friday night is spent eating takeout and letting the smooth sultry voice of the closest thing white people have to Barry White describe a series of unfortunate events until we both pass out from a week's worth of work exhaustion. I have often wondered what gave rise to this interest in two hours of true crime drama, but mostly I like to watch *Dateline* as a gentle reminder to be thankful I am not on it.

GTFO

The fact there is a *Sesame Street* character with obvious anger management issues helps prepare children to deal with parents before the caffeine hits or as it begins to wear off. Thanks, *Sesame Street*. My kids can track my moods far more effectively because of you.

LIKE ME FOR WHO I PRETEND TO BE ⟶

Being liked for any reason is hard enough. But the fact I put so much work into creating a likable facade, much in the way those handy Property Brothers rehab a home to create a series of momentous reveals, deserves a modicum of your appreciation. No?

THIS IS MY GARRY SHANDLING CUP MY TRIBUTE TO GARRY SHANDLING CUP THIS IS WHAT I MADE THE MOMENT I HEARD THE SAD NEWS

enjoy is extremely hot.
consumer recycled fiber.

@YOYOHA

The first time I saw *It's Garry Shandling's Show* it kind of broke my brain. When it comes to TV sitcoms, my love of the artform started with reruns of *Gilligan's Island*, *Three's Company* and *The Brady Bunch* every day after school. Then, as I got older it evolved to *The Cosby Show*, *Family Ties*, *Cheers*, *Night Court* and eventually *Seinfeld*, *The Office*, *Parks and Recreation*, *Community*, *Schitt's Creek*, *Fleabag* and so many others.

It's Garry Shandling's Show took that typical sitcom format and smashed it into a thousand pieces and reassembled them into the comedy equivalent of a cubist painting. I was floored. It was the first time I remember seeing something that just felt completely original. Something that played by the rules it wanted to, then wilfully threw the rest out the window.

Soon after that, my taste in comedy started to change. Sure, Must See TV Thursdays were still must see, but my freshman year in high school, I started watching old *Monty Python* reruns, *The Young Ones* on MTV and movies like *Harold and Maude*, *This Is Spinal Tap* and *Raising Arizona*.

Garry Shandling was the first person that showed me that art can be anything you want it to be. It still has to be good, of course. But you don't have to make the same choices or push yourself through the same Play-Doh barbershop set everyone else is. It's a harder path to take, as most of the people paying for art still want it to match their couch most of the time. But occasionally a great thing like *It's Garry Shandling's Show* sneaks through, changes everything and makes it a bit easier for everyone else who wants to try something new.

So, while 2016 removed a lot of celebrities from the game board, when Garry Shandling died it was so clear how profound an impact he'd made, not only on the comedy world but my own sense of humour. So, I made a cup to the tune of one of the greatest sitcom themes of all time.

#TBT ⟶

As I continue to watch the skin on my face gather up like so many unfolded piles of laundry, I look at raisins with a little more compassion than I used to. Because I too remember the good ol' days when my face was full of life and bursting with fruit flavour.

FOLLOW SOMEONE ELSE'S DREAMS

In the froth of ridiculousness that went into the Republican Party's eventual nomination of the most flawed human being imaginable to represent them in the November election, we were also afforded a shtickle of cringe from the potential First Lady during her speech at the Republican National Convention. Because three passages of her speech felt extremely similar to one given by Michelle Obama the year prior. In an effort to quell the noise, Sean Spicer argued that things My Little Pony's Twilight Sparkle had said about 'following one's dreams' could also be construed as plagiarism. In the whirlwind of inanity, this cup was born.

APRIL FOOLS

Being a social media maven means when the topic of conversation shifts to a scheduled holiday, you better have your shit together when it comes to posting something relevant. Though I must admit, there is a small part of my personality that rejects anything everyone else is doing, so I usually drag my heels on these types of post because hasn't it all been said and done already?

COFFEE IS LIKE A WARM SHOWER FOR YOUR BRAIN

@YOYOHA

Decaf

Shots

Syrup

Milk

...to enjoy is extremely hot.
...post-consumer recycled fiber.

As summertime rolled on, those of us in Ohio were treated to a rare sporting success, seeing LeBron James double-handedly lead the Cleveland Cavs to an impossible 3–1 comeback finals win against Steph Curry's seemingly unstoppable Golden State Warriors.

Now sports, as a subject, don't make their way onto the cups much. My audience has never really been into it, despite the fact that the world could be ending and if there is even the hint of discussion about a notable athlete being traded it would still beat hellfire raining down from the skies as a trending topic on Twitter.

But this moment was special. The look LeBron made after blocking one of Curry's layups in Game 6 released the frustration over every snide comment made at Cleveland's expense over the last six decades.

I am not from Cleveland originally, but my wife is and that's where we started our life together. And because my children were born there, they have no choice but to root for Cleveland sports teams. Lady Macbeth would have an easier time trying to rub out that damn spot than for my children to remove the tattoo of ongoing professional sports shame included with every Cleveland-issued birth certificate.

But this time, in June of 2016, LeBron brought one home. And, unfortunately for them, my kids were at sleepaway camp and missed the whole thing.

From the NBA finals to the 2016 Olympics. I know I just said sports don't usually make their way onto the cups, but you know as well as I do that the Olympics are a different animal.

For one thing, absence makes the heart grow fonder, so the scarcity alone makes them tremendously watchable when they roll back into our lives every four years. Additionally, most of the events are these outsized exaggerations of normal kid stuff: swimming, diving, running, jumping over shit or just dancing around your living room waving around a ribbon on a stick. So, there aren't volumes of complicated rules you need to understand to appreciate them. You want to see how far some gal can throw a spear? Or how fast this guy can backstroke across the pool? Done.

And for events where athletes aren't evaluated by some form of quantitative measurement, like distance, height or speed, a more qualitative assessment must be made. Overnight we are transformed from our mild-mannered workaday selves to the foremost experts on the balance beam and just how many tenths of a point will be deducted due to an unfortunately timed wobble. We are able to take in each performance, then find out just how close we are to being able to list 'Uneven Bars Judge' on our LinkedIn profile.

On 29 August, Gene Wilder, another icon who played a starring role in the development of my sense of humour, died at the age of eighty-three. I adored this man throughout my childhood and still find my way to watching *Willy Wonka* at least three or four times a year.

I am giving this cup full-page billing, but I would be lying if I told you I was happy with the way this came out. It's funny when you're making stuff for the internet; you don't really have time to hone things and get them exactly how you want them to be. When something momentous happens, it's as if my inner voice transforms into Emilio Estévez's dad in *The Breakfast Club*: 'YOYOHA, YOU'VE GOT TO BE NUMBER ONE! I WON'T TOLERATE ANY LOSERS IN THIS FAMILY! YOUR INTENSITY IS FOR SHIT! WIN! WIN! WIN!' The race to make a creative relic to mark the moment is real. I couldn't possibly post about it the next day. By then everyone will be talking about something else and you look late to the wake.

It's not about getting the maximum amount of likes after a tragedy. At least for me it isn't. It's always been more about taking the time to lay something on the digital shrine, along with everyone else's tweets, messages and tributes.

The morning of 8 November, I walked into that voting booth so excited. Excited to move on from the contentiousness of the 2016 race. Excited to go from the first Black president to the first female president. Excited my children were growing up in the most progressive time in our nation's history.

I made all three of these cups that day. I couldn't concentrate on work or anything else. And even though my cartoon Hillary was terrible, I wasn't going to beat myself up over it. It was the dawn of the second new day in eight years and I was ready for it.

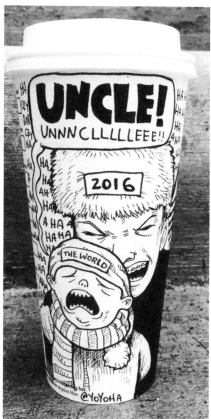

Then, it happened. He won. He fucking won. The feeling I had that night was the same sadness, the same despair I felt on September 11th. But this time, America flew the planes into itself. And what's worse, less than half of the voting public wanted this to happen.

Cartoonists, comedians and intellects of all types would get our shots in, but that November, we knew it was going to be rough. However, I don't think any of us could have possibly conceived just how bad this self-inflicted gunshot wound to our democracy would really be.

JESUS FUCKING CHRIST, 2016, JUST END ALREADY

As the holiday season marched on, and children became ravenously obsessed with another toy that instantly became useless after the first fifteen minutes of ownership, another unthinkable death occurred. Carrie Fisher, the woman responsible for a whole generation of tween boys hitting puberty at the exact same time thanks to a gold bikini, passed away after experiencing a cardiac arrest on a flight home from London.

She was such an incredible human being and represented so much more than the nerdiest sexual fantasy of all time. She was funny, a formidable writer, and one of the first major celebrities to be vocal about her struggles with mental health. And that is just one tenth of one per cent of all the amazing things about her.

Like so many of the wonderful people that died over the course of the shittiest fucking year imaginable, her death was a proverbial twist of a knife that had been repeatedly plunged into every chamber of our hearts on a weekly basis.

Three days later, 2016 was over. We were free. Or so we thought.

2017

NEVER
NOT TIRED

When the final puff of 2016's toxicity cleared, the reality of a Donald Trump presidency started to sink in. Looking back, with the knowledge of what transpired in the years that followed, to go from Barack Obama to Donald Trump is as bad a case of ideological whiplash that has existed in the history of ever.

I look at these men and see two distinct sides of America. One brimming with the sheer greatness of everything this country has to offer its people and its people have to offer their country. A man that not only worked his way up to the world's most powerful office, but once in it, carried himself with the utmost class, style and respect we've ever seen. No scandals, no serious investigations, no indictments. Just a man trying his best to make the country a better place for all of us.

And then you have Donald Trump. A man who embodies all of America's worst, most despicable qualities. A schoolyard bully insulated by his father's wealth and success. A man who speaks with a vocabulary of maybe 100 words in total, all of which are used to denigrate others in an effort to make him feel better about himself.

But this was January of 2017. There was still hope then. Hope that his complete incompetence would somehow save the day and see him removed from office before we slid headfirst into a fascist state.

NEVER NOT TIRED

extremely hot.
recycled fiber

@YOYOHA

DON'T GO, O

This is how so many of us felt. Maybe this cup would have been better if I had replaced myself with the Statue of Liberty, a bald eagle or some other American symbol, but my heart was too broken to see outside my own personal grief. Also it was so hard to recreate the 'O' logo on the cup, I was completely frustrated and not thinking big picture. I am not a political cartoonist and at times like this it shows.

WOMEN'S MARCH

On 21 January, women from all over this country, in numbers far exceeding Trump's inauguration attendance, flew to Washington DC in preparation for a long fucking four years for women's rights. The self-proclaimed pussy-grabbing lout was going to know what he was up against from day one. Watching my friends and family members who were able to attend made me really want to contribute something to the fight. I created this cup to commemorate their courage, their fire and the fight in each and every woman brave enough to stand up for themselves, for each other and for all girls that haven't been born yet.

THE ENVIRONMENTAL IMPACT OF A TRUMP PRESIDENCY
RUSSIAN HACKERS
WHAT IF I'M NOT AS CUTE AS I THINK I AM
ISIS
NEW YEAR, NEW FEARS
@YOYOHA

PISS TRUMP

This is a deep cut for my artist friends. I'll never forget when famed photographer Andres Serrano had an exhibit in Ohio, a few years after famously presenting his controversial *Piss Christ* to the world in 1987. So, after all the alleged rumours of Trump's pee tape, it felt apropos to reimagine the famous photo with someone who might actually like being submerged in tinkle.

STAY WOKE

While I try to remain woke at all times, especially now, there is something funny about that coming from a cup of coffee. Admittedly, the message would have a far greater impact from a locally sourced reusable coffee mug, filled with fair-trade organic coffee made by a company that contributes a portion of their profits to fighting poverty and injustice in coffee-producing nations across the globe. Next time.

ME: GOING TO GET COFFEE
WIFE: YOU CAN'T THERE'S AN ICE STORM OUT THERE.
ME:

SKITCH SKITCH

COFFEE

THE MOST IMPORTANT MEAL OF THE DAY

@YOYOHA

WHEN YOU'RE IN A MEETING AT 4:30 PM ON FRIDAY SLOWLY DYING INSIDE

@YOYOHA

WHAT IN CAFFEINATION

@YOYOHA

SPRINKLE BAE

This world of ours doesn't stay still for very long. There is always a new ridiculous something or other calmly floating atop the terrifying churn of politics, climate change, gun violence and other world calamities. And, to give us a welcome break from the constant hand-wringing that was the first few months of 2017, Salt Bae, the red-meat-slicing Turkish prince, was delivered to distract us from our deepest fears and social concerns for at least a few weeks, adding himself to the globally collected and ever-increasing library of one-GIF wonders that give us a snorkel full of fresh air as we attempt to wade through the rest of the day's news.

LA LA LAND

The 'barista misspelling your name' gag has served me well over the years, but this quick rendition was executed in record time in an effort to ride the conversational wave of the most delightful fuck-up in Oscars history. Faye Dunaway and Warren Beatty were on stage set to announce Best Picture, but instead of forgettably doing their job, Beatty had mistakenly been given a duplicate of the Best Actress envelope (which had been awarded to Emma Stone for *La La Land*). After opening the envelope, instead of announcing the obvious mix-up, he did what most men would do: looked confused, kept his mouth shut and passed the buck to the person standing next to him. Problem was, as soon as Faye Dunaway saw the words '*La La Land*' on the card, she just blurted it out for the entire movie-watching world to hear. And scene.

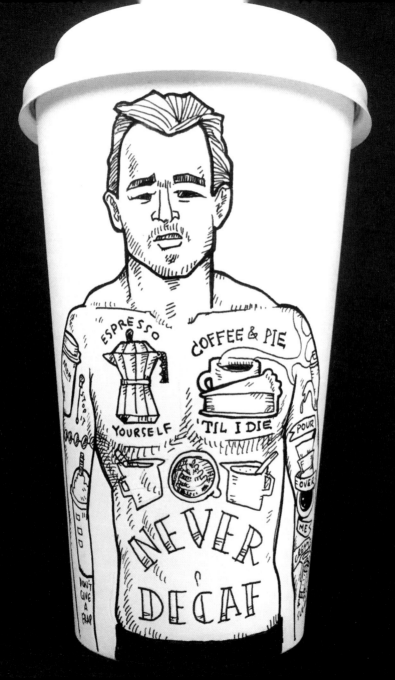

UNICORN FRAPP

Sometimes the mad scientists in the Starbucks lab go a bit too far. While largely hailed by middle schoolers everywhere, this nightmare in whipped food colouring was apparently dyeing the fingertips of baristas everywhere, and was an overall hassle to make. Food art is pain, baristas. Suck it up and make my obnoxious drink.

RICKLES ⟶

While celebrity deaths slowed a bit in 2017, we still lost a few big names. And, even in death, Don Rickles got one last shot off at my expense. One last roast on a Pike Place Roast. I can totally hear his voice when I read it, too. Thus, I will continue to pretend this particular coffee burn was delivered by the legend himself.

I get a lot of shit any time I post anything about Trump. Not an immeasurable amount and nothing compared to my female peers, but it's definitely an easy way to purge a thicket of thorny followers and hear people whine that I 'should stick to making funny cups and leave the politics out of it'. In all honesty, I get that. We all want spaces in our lives that are unaffected by the vitriol we are faced with everywhere else. But at the same time, the human crotch rot of this man and his parade of cronies gleefully eroding our democracy cannot be ignored. So, just because some people's fears are simultaneously stoked and soothed by him doesn't mean the rest of us are going to line up and lick the boot of a mentally ill, racist tyrant.

CUP O' THRONES

Throughout the years I have considered doing more cups inspired by the sheer tonnage of hours spent ravenously consuming all forms of televised entertainment, but for some reason they rarely come to pass. Season seven of *Game of Thrones* was the exception due to its weekly release and communal watch party every Sunday night at 10 p.m. That said, having been force-fed the scripture of the Church of Spoiler Alert, each week I decided it best to leave specific plot points out of this series of cups, instead focusing on more general takes on characters and situations from old seasons.

One development you'll notice in the coming pages is that I started to experiment with a new technique of colourising the cups digitally. Because after 250 of these babies it felt important to keep mixing it up and try new things. Plus it's faster, I like the overall boldness and I can clean up some of the pencil marks while I'm at it.

BAD CASE OF THE HUMANS ⟶

It's funny to think how much better the earth had it when giant monster lizards were crawling all over its surface. Sure, the landscape paintings and television shows have gotten much better since we arrived, but everything else – like the constant stream of carbon emissions and the incarceration of some of nature's most majestic beasts so we can mash our greasy foreheads into sheets of Plexiglas as we ogle them – feels like a rough price to pay for Mother Earth. In fact, Agent Smith from *The Matrix* comparing us to a virus wasn't too far off, especially when you watch reality television or look at satellite images of Los Angeles. So, while I know our days are numbered and the dinosaurs will eventually be able to scream, 'SCOREBOARD, YA WALKING UPRIGHT HAIRLESS BITCHES!' from the afterlife, I take a little solace in turning a small relic of non-biodegradable landfiller into something worth liking on Instagram.

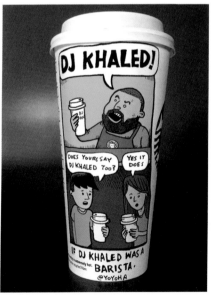

MONTUESDAY

In the *Avengers* movie of our everyday lives, Montuesday is the villain that insidiously lifts its ugly maw over our bedsides the day after a Monday holiday, and figuratively whacks us over the head with a blackjack. Like Hannibal Lecter resting underneath the recently removed face of one of his victims, Montuesday patiently waits for us to realise that the extra day off just gives twice the amount of emails and work meetings to parse through and with one less day to accomplish everything we needed to accomplish for the week. The only way to defeat him is with copious amounts of heart-vibrating coffee.

SO WHAT ARE YOU UP TO TODAY BESIDES BEING AWESOME?
JARIS
@YOYOHA

THIS ONE IS FOR JARIS

A few years ago a barista named Jaris started working at my neighbourhood Starbucks. On his first day, right after taking my order, he brightly asked me, 'What are you up to today, anything fun?' Of course, it being just a random weekday morning, and me, unprepared for any and all human interactions while in line, grumbled, 'Yeah, just heading to work.' The very next day, Jaris greeted me with the exact same question. And again, I replied, 'Just going to work,' slightly annoyed that I should be expected to have a better answer than that.

But, over the next week, and the months that followed, my icy attitude towards Jaris's cheeriness began to thaw and I started to work harder to see what was fun about the upcoming day. His relentless positivity and constant reminders that 'you can do it, I believe in you' made me look forward to seeing him in the morning. He had this innate ability to let me see my day through his eyes, eyes unencumbered by the lazy negativity I tend to bring with me everywhere else.

He has since moved halfway across the country en route to a life outside of our neighbourhood Starbucks. And as I waited to give him this little token to remember us by, every single person in line talked to him about his impending trip and wished him well.

The lesson is and has always been this: you get out of life what you put into it. So no matter where life takes Jaris, I know his future will be bright – because he seizes every single opportunity to make it that way.

Why do I love October so much? Simple. There is nothing more lovely than hearing the giggles of a child rolling around in a crunchy pile of leaf corpses. But more than that, it's an entire month dedicated to the celebration of death. An opportunity to take a long look at the bone puppet inside each and every one of us and say, 'One day I'll just be you, and that's OK.' Some might find it macabre, but for me, having fun with our inevitable demise is one of the healthiest ways to deal with it.

THANKS, FACEBOOK

I have never seen a therapist or dealt with my raging ocean of fears, my constant self-loathing or literally dozens of other issues I carry around with me on a daily basis. But who cares because I can go on social media and pretend I'm A-OK! And hopefully someone else who is suffering will see that my life is terrific and use that as inspiration to stop feeling so down in the dumps!

Another December, another chapter in the *Star Wars* saga. This time revealing the long-awaited origins of blue milk and introducing the SACRED JEDI TEXTS! before making us watch them burn. Which is exactly how I feel about the general universe-meddling that has happened with George Lucas, Steven Spielberg, J. K. Rowling and anyone else who once created something sacred and perfect that we all fell in love with. Don't get me wrong, I still go see them as I love any reason to get out of my house to sit in the dark and eat Milk Duds, but sometimes when the fans who grew up with the movies start being in charge of making new ones, the overall narrative starts to get distorted. It's not the expansion of a new universe, rather one folding over on itself. And sometimes that leads to the occasional deformity. And sometimes, after seeing said films, a few of us quietly retreat to a safe space and scream like Luke did when he found out Darth Vader was his father. A totally normal reaction, I'm told.

THE BEST OF THE REST

After four years, 117,000 followers on Instagram, and god knows how many cups (I could count them but who has the time, this book is already a year overdue), I find myself in the constant mental tango of whether or not people still find this charming, or are quietly humouring me because they feel sorry for anyone who will forever be known in certain internet circles as 'the coffee cup guy'. Nevertheless, I persist and continue to justify all these cups taking up valuable storage space in my basement.

As I get ready to delve into this book's denouement, I must admit this process, this look back at how I've spent a considerable amount of my free time, has made me proud. Most of the time when I reflect on my work, it's accompanied by a general wave of embarrassment and/or a full body cringe. But this has been different. I see more good than bad. I see that my desperation for internet likes got me drawing again. I see countless examples of me doing my best to make people laugh, or think, or think about why they're laughing, or laugh about why they're thinking. I see this little corner of the internet I've carved out that is all my own. Sure, there are other people drawing on coffee cups (I know because every time a person discovers one they send it to me and I feel like I need to challenge them to a sword fight like the movie *Highlander* and once victorious I could scream, 'THERE CAN BE ONLY ONE!' over their decapitated body.*) Of course there is also an abundance of great artists drawing webcomics. But as far as I know, not too many people have combined the two. So maybe, just maybe, in a world where original thoughts are like unicorns, I was able to find one of my very own.

* In *Highlander* the only way for an immortal to kill another immortal is by cutting their head off. Gruesome, I know.

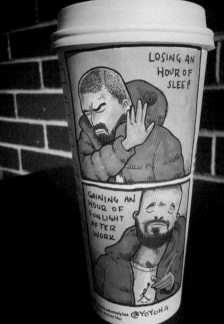

R.I.P. STEPHEN HAWKING

When the smartest man on earth turns back into stardust, you best be pulling out all the stops. He taught us so much about black holes, and not just the ones residing in my own sense of self-worth.

OFFICIAL PORTRAIT →

When Obama unveiled his portrait for the National Gallery, the internet was aglow. While coffee never served as president of the United States, it definitely has served several of them and that's pretty much the same thing.

Clearly movies have played a recurring role in my own personal *Lawrence of Arabica* (ooh, that's good, I should make that cup) because, like coffee itself, a movie is a shared experience from which I can borrow intellectual property when I don't have an original thought in my head. Which is most of the time if I am being honest. And that's OK. Sometimes a more creative person is the perfect springboard to unlocking some other aspect of your own artistic voice. At least that's what I tell myself.

APRIL (SNOW) SHOWERS

When you live in the Midwest, April snow showers usually occur after a few 65°F days have completely convinced you that winter is dead and buried and it's safe to put all your bulkiest fleeces into a few of those vacuum-sealed bags and stack them under your bed like sandwich meats. For our avian brothers and sisters returning from points south, I imagine the awakening is ruder than whatever 'woe is us' emotions we are experiencing. After all, turn the heat back on, throw a blanket over the heat register and you're good to go. This little guy, on the other wing, not so much.

Over the years, some of my most popular cups have featured the animation of the inanimate. Not like Bugs Bunny animation, more like Dr Frankenstein breathing life into a hulking corpse with a disturbing pallor kinda animation. For as long as I can remember, whenever I'm drawing random things like the condiments at my favourite diner while I wait for my two eggs over medium, wheat toast, hash browns with cheese and onions and a single pancake (for breakfast dessert), the finishing touch has always been making them say stuff. What would salt shaker say if it could? (Probably something like, 'Put me on your bacon, let's see what happens.')

While this corner of my imagination has served my comics well, it also has its side effects. For instance, I am a person that feels bad if I put all the clean plates from the dishwasher on top of the single plate in the cabinet because dammit, it's that plate's turn!

And what if one of the grape tomatoes meant for my lunch salad accidentally rolls off the cutting board and I throw it in the trash? I can't decide if the tomato is happy to escape being eaten or if it's sad that it didn't achieve its purpose in life. So, yeah, an imagination is a good thing to have most of the time, but when it starts pretending everything around you has feelings and a soul and a purpose on this earth it can be a big pain in the ass.

LISTEN ALL Y'ALL IT'S SELF-SABOTAGE

This cup says so much about the constant struggle between the me trying to live a happy and fulfilling life and the other me continually making bad choices because they make me feel good for a few minutes, or in the case of eating too many M&Ms, a few seconds.

From my perspective, this is the game of life. Not the one where you get to stuff little pegs into a plastic car and try and collect gobs of paper cash before reaching the finish line. The real one with pain, joy and everything in between.

I don't know why good decisions are so hard to make. But I will keep trying to make them in between late-night snacks.

All this makes me think of the tweet pinned to my Twitter profile:

'When I was young I did stupid things because I didn't know any better. Now I know better and do stupid things because I miss being young.'

So that's it. It's nostalgia's fault. I blame nostalgia.

More celebrity deaths, more tributes lovingly illustrated on disposable coffee cups. While Stan Lee and Aretha Franklin left Earth after living long and fulfilling lives, lives that reached the absolute pinnacle of achievement in their respective fields, Anthony Bourdain was taken from us far too soon.

JACOB FUCKING WOHL

For those who may not know, Jacob Wohl is a hapless conservative dipshit who is willing to say just about anything to get some of that sweet attention nectar to rub on his proverbial gums. After Trump took office, he often took to Twitter to talk about his adventures in eavesdropping in 'hipster coffee shops', often spinning yarns about just how happy mainstream America was with having a narcissistic psychopath running the country. If you want to see unbridled idiocy in action, just google him. You won't be disappointed.

Living in a world in which stupid people can make decisions that negatively impact the health of others is one of the most maddening aspects of modern life. Despite the fact that human ingenuity has been engineering solutions to problems since cavemen developed tools, at some point in human history there was a divergence, and we decided to base our societies on the moral framework of religion instead of science. This shift left the mysteries of the universe to be explained by fairy tales and invisible beings in the sky

as opposed to research, analysis and facts. Which allows people to believe all sorts of things that are contrary to all the evidence in front of their eyes, ears and faces. Don't get me wrong, I am not anti-religion. I think it has the ability to provide a lot of hope, comfort and community to people all over this earth. But when people use it to betray the hard work of medical science and instead decide to base life and death decisions on something they saw on Facebook, we, as a species, are inevitably going to have problems.

When I was a kid the developers of generally useless products that somehow capture the attention of the general public came up with a simple idea: thought and speech bubble stickers that were meant to be affixed to photographs of your loved ones. They had their moment in the early nineties, despite the fact that developing a roll of film cost somewhere in the neighbourhood of $8,200.* But it was so worth it. I mean, how else could a picture of a puzzled-looking grandmother be transformed into an epic 'who farted' gag? As trite (and hilarious) as that sounds, I see now that this convergence of words and pictures were one-of-a-kind analogue memes.

Shortly thereafter, as the internet was becoming a part of everyday life, Adobe released its first edition of Photoshop. And like a person carrying a chocolate bar colliding with a person carrying an open jar of peanut butter, these two great things became greater together and eventually transformed into an artform that has made a few nitwits into multi-millionaire media conglomerates.

* Cost adjusted for inflation.

When they aren't crashing people's weddings for an unexpectedly fun viral moment on social media, celebrities are out there doing their best to live normal lives. As evidenced in the cup on the near right, where I did my best to capture the viral photo of Jonah Hill's coffee nopeing the fuck out as a cautionary tale to anyone who may have thought holding a full coffee by its lid was a remotely good idea.

And after Chrissy Teigen posted a photo of her and John Legend looking absolutely exhausted in honour of their anniversary, I could not resist doing a coffee-cup version. Not only because they seem to be one of those rare celebrity couples that truly adore one another, but because Chrissy has been following me on Instagram for a while now, which is something I fear even saying out loud because I don't want to put anything in the universe that might correct this obvious mistake. Due to that, she not only saw the cups, but also sent me a DM asking if she could buy them. A request I denied because I really don't like selling my cu— SIKE of course I fucking sold them to her. To think a little part of me may be occupying a random back shelf in their home is mind-blowing. Especially because I loaded a very small tracking device in the cups and will be arriving for an unannounced visit the next time I'm in Los Angeles.

A funny thing happened after this picture of Phoebe Waller-Bridge blazed through the internet after the Emmys. My cousin knows her agents and, long story short, this cup could also be resting on a shelf in her London flat. I had hoped to receive a pic of her and the cup as proof but her aversion to social media has prevented that from happening. Oh well. I suppose the knowledge that she occasionally walks by it on her way to the loo is enough for me. Or that it is comfortably sitting in a box with a bunch of other weird coffee-cup fan art.

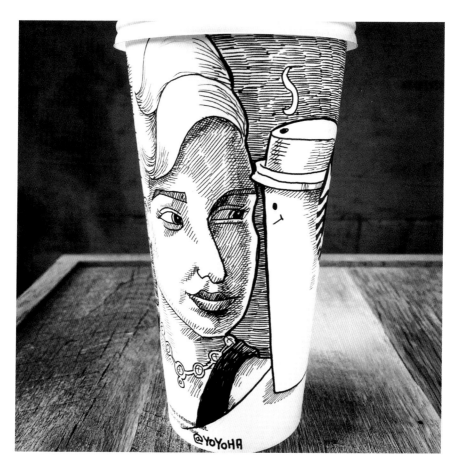

@YOYOHA

Speaking of award shows, remember that time Lady Gaga and Bradley Cooper sang a duet at the Oscars and gazed lovingly into each other's eyes and sent the rumour mill aflame with the thought that they probably definitely obviously must have hooked up during the filming of *A Star Is Born* and then two months later Bradley Cooper broke up with his girlfriend and everyone thought that he and Gaga were going to become a thing but it didn't really happen but we still all felt some gratification that we read their body language correctly?

The final season of *Game of Thrones* came and went, and aside from the fact that a cup of Starbucks made a cameo (and can thus be considered canon in the universe of Westeros), it was widely considered a confusing and insufferable effort by the show runners. But, for six seasons it was a perfect show, and that is still an accomplishment. An accomplishment that pales in comparison to all but destroying what would have been one of the most watched and re-watched series in the history of television. So, move over *Star Wars* fans, there's a new fantasy realm that will forever be a disappointment to its fan base.

SHARPIES GONNA SHARPIE

As hurricane season reared its windswept head, the most loathsome president in the history of America took what looked like a devastating weather report and turned it into another example of just how low his crippling narcissism could sink. At the same time, a random White House Sharpie realised its true potential.

BREW, DAVID

Every once in a while a TV show comes along that, above all else, makes you fall in love with the characters to a level where you truly feel connected to each and every one of them. *Schitt's Creek* is, was and forever will be a gift.

RAPINOE-SHEDIDN'T

Beautiful human Megan Rapinoe began the chase for the Women's World Cup by saying there was no fucking way she would be caught dead in the White House. And our wet-tissue-paper-skinned president, never one to back down from a perceived slight, said she should concentrate on winning the cup first. So they did. And Donald Trump got to look like an asshole idiot fuckwad once more.

Also, the fact that the US Men's National Team makes more money than these women is a crime. They aren't good enough to pick the mud out of these women's cleats.

Work travel doesn't happen too often for me these days, and when it does it has most often been to New York City. But one week during the summer of 2019 I got called in to film a video at an animal shelter in Denver, Colorado.

Luckily, video shoots tend to add a few more travel days just to scout the location, chat with the people we are interviewing and the like, so the day of the shoot will have fewer surprises. Well, that extra day comes with a sizable chunk of free time, so having never been to Denver, I took the opportunity to travel up to Red Rocks. I grabbed a few pens, a blank coffee cup and took a Lyft to the storied amphitheatre. And because no lack of a plan goes unpunished, right as I arrived the announcement came over the PA that all lollygaggers had to split so they could get ready for the evening's concert (paraphrasing). But, being the first-world anarchist that I am, I was able to make my way through a blockade to throw a quick eye on it before an usher chased me out with a push broom. (That didn't actually happen, but she did politely ask me to leave which is pretty much the same thing.)

On my way out of there, I asked another usher if I could hike down to Morrison, the town just at the base of Red Rocks, and she looked at me like I was a crazy person. I took that as a 'yes' and plugged Morrison into Apple Maps and found a route which involved walking down the side of the road like a stranded motorist looking for a gas station. Thankfully, the road was windy enough that most of the cars driving by were easy to detect and avoid, even though I was blasting Sigur Rós in my AirPods in an attempt to establish a spiritual connection with the landscape. Like taking peyote, but without the vomiting and hallucinations.

It was a delightful little hike. Downhill for the most part, and surrounded by these bright rock formations shouting out from the greenery like a pack of sports fans trying to catch a free t-shirt. After about forty-five minutes I arrived in downtown Morrison. And when I say 'downtown' it's really just a strip of restaurants, gift shops and of course, Morrison Joe, a coffee shop where I was able to bathe in a cold blast of air conditioning, sip on an Americano and get this cup underway.

In short, it was a perfect Denver afternoon with my little buddy.

#NATIONALCOFFEEDAY

A funny thing happened after five straight years of drawing cartoons on hundreds of Starbucks cups. Starbucks actually called. And when I say called I mean they reached out via a well-known influencer platform. They wanted a few cups for the upcoming #NationalCoffeeDay holiday, which is like the

Yom Kippur of fake internet holidays. I enthusiastically accepted. Did they make me their chief creative cartoon cup officer (CCCCO)? No. But it was tremendously validating to finally get paid to do something I have been doing for free forever. I guess when I think of it that way I am lucky they asked me at all.

THE WAITING

We all do it. Sitting there, trying to maintain our composure amidst a churning sea of coffee-shop patrons, all patiently waiting for their drinks of all shapes and sizes.

Most of the time I keep my face buried in my phone with an eye pointed towards the chorus line of finished drinks on the carryout ledge, but sometimes I put away the phone, and watch the countless number of behavioural rituals on display.

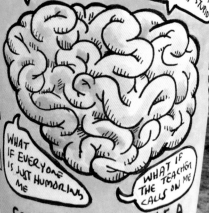

The dumbest president to ever suck oxygen into his Adderall-dusted lungs got impeached – because he's a moron rich kid that never had to suffer the consequences of his actions even once in his disgusting life. So when he attended a World Series game in Washington and got booed incessantly? That felt good.

BABY YODA

And just when things seemed their bleakest, Disney did what Disney was always going to do with the *Star Wars* universe. It gave birth to a tiny, adorable Force-using green baby for us to have, and eventually hold (in $39.99 plush toy form). Enjoy your blue milk latte, little buddy.

You know that scene in the first *Harry Potter* movie where he goes to Ollivanders wand shop and he tries a couple of wands but every time he gives them a wave something weird and/or terrible happens and then Ollivander goes back into the stacks and whispers to himself, 'I wonder…' before grabbing a wand, and when Harry holds that wand in his hand he is enveloped by a golden light and his hair sticks up like when that kid from your fourth-grade class put his hand on the static electricity orb at your local science museum?

That.

That's what drinking coffee is like.

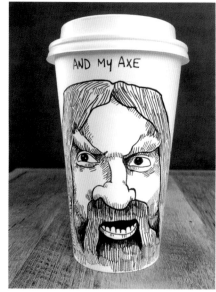

And that's it. This is the part of this story where there is, in fact, an end. It's not to say I'll never draw something on the side of a coffee cup again, because I'm sure I will when the moment feels right (plus I have a huge box of blank paper cups in my basement crying out to be vandalised). It's more like, now that this book is finally done, I don't feel like I have to anymore. I can search for the next idea that might make my Instagram account worth following. I mean, I have barely scratched the surface of other disposal products that might take ink fairly well. Perhaps paper plates will be next, or some inexpensive plastic stemware.

But it was never about the cups really. It's about taking some time every day, or every other day, or perhaps every third day, to sit down, pop in my AirPods, and draw something while I listen to reruns of *The Office* on Netflix. To pull some funny thought out of the constant news-feed ticker inside my brain and make it into something I can share and see if other people find it as funny as I do. And that, my friends, is the healthiest use of my time that doesn't require athletic wear, physical strain and sobbing.

Because making stuff is always worthwhile. As my most favourite author of all time, Kurt Vonnegut, once wrote to a group of high school students:

> Practise any art, music, singing, dancing, acting, drawing, painting, sculpting, poetry, fiction, essays, reportage, no matter how well or badly, not to get money and fame, but to experience becoming, to find out what's inside you, to make your soul grow.

This book is not setting out to be a *New York Times* bestseller. When I look back, now that I'm at the end of my coffee-cup era, I see that its reason for being is merely to prove that I was able to find a group of people that appreciated me enough to make this book happen. And for that, I will be forever grateful.

EPILOGUE

This was not part of the original manuscript, but a lot has happened since I finished writing this book. And I'm fairly convinced a lot more is set to happen between now and its release in 2022.

At the time of writing, I have been holed up in my home for ten straight months. I have not been inside a store, a restaurant or (most painfully) a movie theater in almost a year. No trip to the office, no birthday celebration, no holiday or well attended gathering of any kind. The only reasons I leave my house these days are to walk the dogs, drop off an insane quantity of empty cardboard boxes at the community recycling bin a few miles away, or to drive to my parents' house for a masked-up and distanced visit on their new, Covid-friendly patio.

And, honestly, no other human being in the history of lockdowns and quarantines has been more mentally prepared for this. In fact, I'm perfectly content to stay in and putter around my house for another decade if I have to. My biggest concern these days is how long I can keep this going after the nation is vaccinated and herd immunity is achieved. Like, how long will I feasibly be able to use Covid as an excuse not to attend things I'm invited to? How long will I be able to avoid looking nice, and when will I be forced to wear clothes without visible stains again?

Before the pandemic, I used to have a lot of good shirts with a variety of cooking-related food stains on them – shirts I could never wear out in public without looking like someone who was clearly down on their luck. Why was I holding on to them? Quarantine, baby. You can't see shirt stains on a Zoom call, and even if you could we all know that everyone spends 90 per cent of every video conference not inspecting our co-workers' choice of outfits, but instead looking at our own slightly puffed-up and rapidly aging faces. It's horrifying, really. Like a car wreck that you can't help but slow down and look at.

You know the reason that people slow down to look at car wrecks? It's the same reason people love true crime and watching *Dateline* on Friday nights. It's not because people love tragedy. It's because people love to see the tragedies they have avoided being a part of. It helps us cope with the mini-tragedies we experience every day, like when you hear your dog dry-heaving and you rush them to the door, and right before you turn the knob, the dog throws up all over the doormat instead of on the wooden floor that would be far easier to clean. Yes, that sucks, but at least my wife isn't slowly poisoning me by putting rare toxic chemicals in my sandwiches.

OK. I'm straying from the point of this epilogue. I wanted to write it because so much has changed since the early days of the project when I could joyfully scribble on a coffee cup and post it on Instagram without a care in the world. The last year has helped me realise just how manic and unhappy the world of social media was making me.

Every week, I was desperately trying to make time to draw on cups just so I could send a handful of posts into the digital ether. I pressured myself to keep growing the account, and was crestfallen each time a cup underperformed. I was immensely frustrated to see my cartoonist friends easily eclipse ten or twenty thousand likes on every post. I felt betrayed by the algorithm; or worse, I felt that the thing that sounded so funny in my head wasn't actually funny at all, and that this gimmick of drawing on coffee cups was the only reason I was able to attract an audience to begin with. You know, the typical abuse our brains are so adept at shovelling onto our already slumped shoulders.

And then, as Tom Hanks says in the movie *Cast Away*, 'a feeling came over me like a warm blanket'.

Let me preface said feeling by informing you that throughout my entire life I have wanted this, drawing cartoons, to be my job. So, this Instagram account was 100 per cent going to be my ticket to book deals, a line of signature plush coffee cups, an animated series that would outrun *The Simpsons* or, most realistically, a six-figure job at Starbucks drawing a daily coffee cup comic that would be published on that web page that pops up when you log on to their free Wi-Fi. Every post became the pull on the handle of a slot machine with the chance of fame and fortune on the other end. Finally, I would be able to show my wife and kids that my lack of presence in their lives for nearly a decade was totally worth it, that all this time on the couch mastering the art of drawing on a curved surface wasn't for naught.

But in reality, what dawned on me was that this Instagram account is just a fun hobby. It's never going to be anything more than that. And that's OK.

I started thinking of my creative life this way: in the world of food, there are all kinds of restaurants. There are Michelin star-having, James Beard Award-winning establishments that are respected across the globe. There are major chains you can find in every town across the country, and hugely popular fast-food joints. And then there are these local dives that may not be much to look at, and that not too many people even know about, but where you can get a great and memorable meal nonetheless.

I am totally fine being one of those dive restaurants. Because it's not about fame and fortune; it's about making the things you are good at making, and finding people who appreciate them just as much as they do the fancy mega-talents.

If I wanted the Michelin-starred life so badly, I would have worked harder at it. I wouldn't have consistently taken no for an answer. But all along, I knew the cartoonist's life was a difficult one. Instead, I chose to use my creativity in the most commercially viable way I could: graphic design, copywriting, art directing, content strategising. Creative work that came with health benefits, talented co-workers, client presentations and occasional work travel that allowed me to stay at the Four Seasons in downtown St Louis.

Basically, I sold out. But – and this cannot be understated – I am so thankful I was lucky enough to have something to sell. I guess what I'm trying to say is that for the first time ever I am unencumbered by regret. Unencumbered by self-loathing for not finishing the movie script or developing the TV show or achieving all the things I thought I wanted to achieve or making all the things I wanted to make.

Today, I make things because I want to, not because I feel like I have to. And if I keep losing followers every time I post, or a particular comic only gets a thousand likes instead of five or six thousand, I could give a shit. I am not saving the world, or myself, or trying to use these comics for any other purpose than to hopefully make someone's day a touch brighter.
So, while I may still draw on a cup for old times' sake, this book, this collection of every ridiculous thought and idea that percolated through my over-caffeinated brain during those five years, is my swansong, allowing me to place a coffee drip-shaped period at the end of this Venti Pike Place-sized sentence.

I'd still take that job at Starbucks, though.

ACKNOWLEDGEMENTS

I know this section of the book is typically used to acknowledge the people who helped make it a reality, and I will do that as well, but first I wanted to acknowledge something else.

This book has come out about two years later than I thought it would. So, to all the people who waited patiently, all the supporters who pledged money to help make this book happen, thank you. Thank you for buying an expensive ticket to get a front-row seat to my never-ending, prone-to-distraction, desperate-to-please, terrified-to-disappoint madness. I know they used to make whole *Star Wars* movies in the same amount of time it took to get this book in your hands. And this is no *Star Wars* movie; there are a lot of *Star Wars* references in it, but not enough to warrant being purchased by Disney.

To those who waited so long, I sincerely hope you enjoy it.

I'd also like to acknowledge that I didn't ask anyone to write a foreword for this book, because I hate the idea of giving someone else a creative to-do item, especially with no promise of payment.

And now, the people that really helped this book happen. First, Mark Hoppus, who, when I told him no one was interested in my book, tweeted to his millions of followers about it and attracted the attention of a chap named Craig Beadle, who tagged the Unbound Twitter account into the conversation. Unbound introduced me to Lizzie Kaye, who was responsible for commissioning the book. Thank you, Lizzie: your support and patience were invaluable to my creative process.

I would like to thank all the great people I have worked with over the last ten years, especially the ones who didn't give me a hard time while I scribbled on coffee cups during meetings. I was a freelance graphic designer for a good decade and my whole life trajectory changed when I started working at Resource Interactive (later Resource, then Resource Ammirati: marketing agencies love a good rebrand) in 2011. Thanks to Lora, Marti, Tara, Mark, Joe, Jen, Luke, Iris, Dave, Courtney, Sam, Kit, Brian, Amanda, Dennis, Derrick and to my original team of talented writers: Amy, Chris, Mary Kate, Kelly, Kevin and Daniel.

Thank you to my Tante Cola, who remains one of the funniest people I have ever known. Her ability to joke and make me laugh is probably one of the reasons I fell in love with all forms of comedy at a young age.

I could go on and name pretty much all my cousins at this point, so let me just say, the times I spent with family growing up were some of the happiest of my life.

Thank you to my parents, who loved me even when I was unlovable, pushed me into art school and made creativity part of my everyday life. And thank you to my brother Jesse: our shared passion for comedy, movies and diner food has made the entirety of our life together so much more enjoyable. I love you all too much.

Thank you to my wife Halle, to whom this book is dedicated, and my sons Jonah and Izzy. I would like to acknowledge that I probably haven't been the best dad or husband with all my scribbling on coffee cups, staring at my phone and constant searching for some creative rabbit hole to dive into. Thank you for putting up with all of this. I promise I will try to grow up and act like an adult someday soon. Not too soon. But within the next twenty years or so. I love you all. Don't hold me to the twenty years thing.

And finally, coffee. None of this would have been possible without you. I could have chosen a healthy lifestyle and used exercise and eating right to fill me with clean, wholesome energy, but because I'm a bad decision factory, that would never have been a realistic solution. So, it's you. It's always been you. My reason to get up. My reason to stay up. My reason to believe in myself. I love you, coffee. Forever and always.

Unbound is the world's first crowdfunding publisher, established in 2011.

We believe that wonderful things can happen when you clear a path for people who share a passion. That's why we've built a platform that brings together readers and authors to crowdfund books they believe in – and give fresh ideas that don't fit the traditional mould the chance they deserve.

This book is in your hands because readers made it possible. Everyone who pledged their support is listed below. Join them by visiting unbound.com and supporting a book today.

Raj Choudhary	Emily Elliott	Afton Ginlock	Christine Harvell
Skye Christakos	Kristy Elliott	Dave Gisborn & Lani	Becky Hass
Angie Chubb	Cindy Elmore	Straus	Amber Hayes
Lisa Chung Bender	Anita Embleton	Gordon Glenn	Kate Henry
Amy Clark	Christa Engquist	Danny Glimcher	Carol and Roy Hermalyn
Alexia Clarke	Spencer and Austin	Lenna Go	Therese Hilleary
Carrie Cobb	Eppstein	Eric Gohs	Mark Hillman
Eric Coffey	Carlos Espinoza	Bonnie Gold	Calista Ho
Mark Coffey	Bryan Espiritu	Brandy Goldberg	Amanda Hocking
Samantha Cohen	Alesia Estabrook	Meredith Goldman	Seth Hoffman
Iris Coker	Laura Evans	Nicole Goldsbury	Mark Holz
Molly Collie	Francis F	Elizabeth Goldstein	Erica Meister Hondroulis
Jessica Confessore	Kristy Fairweather	Gen Goodwin	Mark Hoppus
Meg Cook	Therese Falk	G Gopalraj	Mary Hougaard
Heather Cornett	Meizlish Family	Drew Gorman-Lewis	Megan Hoying
Jeanne Cosgrove	Jessica Federico-Taylor	Kirsten Graffeo	Madelyn Hubbard
Mandy Costley	Mackenzie J Ferrante	Beth Grampetro	Klay Huddleston
Bob Courtney	Johanna Finch	Cara Granter	Maxwell Huffman
Astrid Crocker	Chris Finnegan	Sophie Green	Jen Hulme
CrystalLakeManagment	Mark Fisher	Torey Greenwald	Rex Huppke
Nicole Cucci	Tina Folster	Janine Grey	Vanessa Hurtado
Colin Curtis	Shelby Forrester	Lisa Griebling	Cheryl Iacono
Alex Daitch	Jouett Francesca	Douglas Griffith	Maria Iannarino
Athene Damsted	Kristina Francis	Tom Griffiths	Erik Isaacson
Kelley Danyi	McClellan Francis	Robin Grubbs	Rahim Jahit
Matthew Davie	Vicky Frank	Brittany Grunau	Catherine James
Jill Davis	Mary Kate Frietch	Andrea Guerra	Talia Jane
Lara De Lange	Justin Fuchs	Owen Gwilliam	Benjamin Jani
Samantha De Maio	Emily Fuller	Blanche Haddad	Aubree Johnson
Julia DeVillers	Erika Furey	Rosalyn Halford	CJ Johnson
Miss Dina Diaz	Jack Gaede	Ainul Hanafiah	Leanne Johnson
Sarah DiCicco	Regina Gagliardo	Patricia Hanrahan	Jo Jones
Traci-Ann DiSalvatore	Laura Gaines	Donna Hara	Melanie Jones
James Donofrio	Rebecca Gardner	Hani Hara	Tamalé Joy
Katie Doten	Laurel Gaut	Jesse Hara	Sophia Justus
Patrick Dotson	Conor Gentes	Trisha Harp	Jennifer Kahler
Julia Doyle	Babak Ghalebi	Angela Harper	Bodil Kalkman
Nikola Dragovic	Isaac Gilbert	Rachael Harrison	Toshi Kameoka
Caroline Duwors	Jalene and Mike Gilbert	RaeLynne Harrison	Andrea Kammerer
Lisa Dvorak	Kate Gilbreath	Sara Harte	Kyra Kane
The Eachii	Gregor Gilliom	Stacey Hartley	Jessica Kania

Troy Kasper	Ha Li	Amy Mibb	Paulina Paiz-Morales
Aleksandra Kaszowska	Avi Libman	Mark Michaels	Cristina Pallares
Kate InTheStudio	Maddy Lierman	Erm Mics	Susan Parrish
Marina Katherine	Derrick Lin	Jennifer Milacci	Melissa Parsons
Laura Kato	Joselin Linder	Melissa Misthal	Melanie Patridge
Jordan Katterheinrich	Scott Linnen	Brad Mitchell	Christina Patterson
Beth Kaufman	David Livingston	John Mitchinson	Liliana Patton
Kevin Kayse	Alicia Lornas-Gross	Barbara Mohl	Fontine Pedersen
Cathy & Bobby	Jasmine Low	Matthew Mohr	Benjamin Penner
Kellerman	Frank Lowe	Brian Lund Mølgaard	Tawny Perkins
Tressa Kelly	Micaela Lozano	Julia Mondabon	Maggie Perks
Andy Kennemer	Asher M-kirk	Daniel Mondak	Susan Perry Miller
Carolyn Kerr	Victoria Macchia	Judith Montanaro	Michael Pestana
Kendra Ketchmark	Jay Macke	Leandra Montes	Megan Petersen
M. Khan	Michalina Mackowski	Sara Moran	Chris Peterson
Samiksha Khanna	Emmy Maddy Johnston	Lukáš Moser	Joe Petruccio
Erica Kibler-Buchanan	Rachel Madsen	Alana Moshier	Molly Pfister
Dan Kieran	Kelly Maholland	Decker Moss	Philip & Gail
Kara Kirby	David R. Mann	Greg Moss	Jerry Phillips
Josh Klynn	Sarah Mansfield	Ayesha Moughel	Natalie Pilato
Amy Knapp	Dora Marin	Jill Mulder	Nicole Polichano
Jennifer Knee	Kali Marino	Melissa Nandi	Amie Pollack
Michelle Knowles	Mariana Markell	Shelby Nathans	Justin Pollard
Nancy Kramer	Mandy Marlowe	Juliann Nathanson	Whitney Poma
WF Kroll	Melissa Maurer	Jessica Nauman	Jessica Pool
Lauren Kushkin	Rosanna Maxwell	Carlo Navato	David Poole
Whitney Kyle	Jen Mayo	Liz Neeb	Andrew Porter
Laura Lafix	Patrick McAllister	Kelly Nelson	Marti Post
Susie Lambert	Mary McBrien	Meredith Nelson	Katherine Powell
Veronica Landa	Holly McCarley	Sarah Nelson Smith	David Price
Kate Landon	Joseph McCarthy	Deborah Newman	Michael Price
Jeremy Law	Cate McCleery	Ian Newton	Ginger Pullen
David Lawler	Rachelle McDonough	B Ng	Laura Putnam
Britt Lee	Nathan McGavin	Kevin Ng-Tang	Niko R.
Kim Lee	Elsa McLaughlin	Shane Nickerson	Minerva Ranjeet
Michael Lerud	Nadia McLean	Colin Nourie	Ben Ranson
Michael Leslie	Calvin Mcphaul	Mandi OHzee	Clair Raujol
Jay Lessard	Dean J Meester	Guy Opochinski	Kim Rayer
Frank Lesser	Jen Meredith	William Otteman	Scott Razek
Julie F. Levine	Kari Merkel	Lauren and Joey P	Amanda Rearick
Puca Lewnau	Chad Meuse	Ian Padgham	Margaret Regan

Taylor Reid
Dania Reyna
Amy C. Reynolds
J. Reynoso
Kevin Rhodes Tiny
Rebecca Richey
Yoni Riemer
Kris Rivera-Lynn
Elise Robinson
Megumi Robinson
Ronelle Rode
Alexa Rodriguez
Melissa Rodriguez
Will Rodriguez
Joe Rogan
Dustin Rogers
Sarah Roha
Sam Rolf
Bertie Rose
Marty Ross-Dolen
Raquel Rossiter
Ben Row
Richard Ruggerio
Abby Rumpke
Jillian Rupnow
Sean Ryan
Rachel Sabella
Brian Sacca
Jennifer Sacks
Sara Saldoff
Ridley Sandidge
Neeraj Sane
Mike Saucedo
Anne-Marie Schiefer
Lindsey Schindler
Keir Schlatter
Olivia Schow
Mia Schubert
Jay Schulman
Christal Seitz
Chris Serico

Theresa Seybold
Amy Sharp
Cynthia Shaw
Joan Shell
Erika Shemberg
Dan Shust
Elisa Silverglade
Ruth Silverman
Beth amd Rau Silverstein
Sarah Singer-Nourie
Christina Smale
Amber Smith
Cindy Smith
Crystal Smith
Jessica Smith
Philippa Smith
Michelle Smyth
Ruth Ann Sneith
Kim and Adam Snyder
Meity Soenarso
Cola Solwitz
DJ Sosnowski
Ilana Spector
Gena Spires
Stephen Spota
Sanjeevan & Roveena
Srikrishnan
Stacey
Karen Starback
Drew Stark
Steven Steenburgh
Tabatha Stirling
Nadiyah Sulayman
Michael Sullivan
Amberle Suprak
Fiona Sutherland
Keri Swanson
Jenna Tabor
Raha Tajrishi
Mark Talis
Sarah Tanner

Ian Thomas
Kaitlin Thomas
Justin Thompson
Bethanne Tilson
Katie Tilson
Ryan Timmons
Rachel Tobias
Crissy Toft
Rachel Tomasic
Marissa Torio
Diana Tout
Erin Treinen
Todd Troeth
Ricky Trogdon
Connie Tuckerman
Andrew Turner
Mike Turner
Lois Tyler
Stephanie Unson
Katie Vago
Zoe Valentine
Jill Van Beke
Thomas Verleye
Anastasia Vito
Laura Wagner
Masato BJ Wakabayashi
Pat Walker
Ashley Wallace
Jay and Samantha
Walters
Karina W. Ward
Emily Warden
Eric Wasserstrom
Jennifer Weissert
Rebecca Weld
Samantha Wellengard
Jennifer Werner
Kate Wilson
Kristyn Wilson
Tim Wilson
Lora Winning

Puranut Wisutjindaporn
Shawn Wolfe
Chris Wood
Jamie Woodham
Alexander Woolston
D & L Wozney
Steve Wyatt
Lynn Yang
Sara Younes
Jim Young
Ranada Young
Tanya Young
Meredith Yuskewich
Rouslana Zafirova
Vicki Zandbergen
Barry Zeidman
Lisagail Zeitlin
Nancy Zhou
Angel Zimmerman